me no speak
Language Companion

France
France

www.menospeak.com

Me No Speak: France
ISBN 978-0978768041
1st edition–September 2010

Published by
Me No Speak, San Francisco, CA USA
www.menospeak.com
info@menospeak.com

Design & Content: Cheryn Flanagan
Operations & Sales: Benjamin Kolowich
Illustration: Kari Lehr

Copyright ©2010, Me No Speak
All rights reserved

Cover photo by Kimberly Kradel

When you can't say it, point to it.

From transportation glitches to dining disasters—and, yes, bathroom emergencies—our books are the result of difficulties we faced in foreign countries with limited language skills.

It all started one night in a Chinese hotel room, wondering how we could possibly get a train ticket or order food when no one spoke English—we solved the issue with hand-drawn pictures and phrases and it was so successful, we just had to turn the idea into a book. We believe travelers should attempt the language of their destination, but sometimes a picture really is worth a thousand words.

Our books are translated by native speakers, and have been developed from our own personal experience. Happy trails!

General help | pages 4 - 7

Do you need to make a phone call, find the toilet, or do some banking? This catch-all section will help you through simple conversations and everyday needs.

Food & drink | pages 8 - 20

With the picture lexicons and menus in this section, you'll be able to order food easily and communicate special dietary restrictions like food allergies or vegetarian requests.

Getting around | pages 21 - 26

Get there quickly by pointing to your destination: the train station, the airport—even the post office. Also get help with everything from reserving bus tickets to renting a bicycle or finding a mechanic.

Accommodation | pages 27 - 30
Come here for help getting a room, and for questions about checkout time and curfews or requests for an extra blanket, hair dryer, wake-up call, or left luggage.

Shopping | pages 31 - 36
If you've forgotten something at home, or need to stock up on memory cards, batteries, or tooth paste, come here for help communicating your needs to store clerks.

Health & Safety | pages 37 - 40
In the event of health & safety issues, this section will help you with everything from buying aspirin to getting to the hospital, finding a dentist, and reporting lost or stolen items to the police.

Can you find an English-speaker?	**How do you say (in French)...?**
Pouvez-vous trouver quelqu'un qui parle anglais ?	Comment dit-on (en français)... ?
Can you point to it?	**I don't understand**
Pouvez-vous me montrer ?	Je ne comprends pas
Can you write down the word?	**I'd like to hire a translator**
Pouvez-vous m'écrire ce mot ?	J'aimerais embaucher un traducteur
Do you understand?	**May I take a photo?**
Vous comprenez ?	Puis-je prendre une photo ?

GENERAL HELP

I need to make a local phone call
J'ai besoin de passer un appel local

I need to make a long distance phone call
J'ai besoin de passer un appel longue distance

I need to make an international phone call
J'ai besoin de passer un appel international

I need a SIM card for my cell phone
J'ai besoin d'une carte SIM pour mon téléphone mobile

I need a telephone card
J'ai besoin d'une carte téléphonique

I'd like to rent a cell phone
J'aimerais louer un téléphone mobile

GENERAL HELP • TOILET

Toilettes
Toilet

Hommes   Femmes

Men   Women

It's an emergency!   The toilet is clogged
C'est une urgence !   Les toilettes sont bouchées

May I use your bathroom?   Where is the bathroom?
Puis-je utiliser vos toilettes ?   Où se trouvent les toilettes ?

GENERAL HELP • BANKING

Banque
Bank

Cash	Credit card	Money exchange	Travelers checks
Espèces	Carte de crédit	Change	Chèques de voyage

Can you break this note?
Pouvez-vous me faire de la monnaie ?

I need a cash advance
J'ai besoin d'une avance en espèces

I need to make a wire transfer
J'ai besoin de faire un virement

What is the exchange rate?
Quel est le taux de change ?

Heure

Time

Monday Lundi	**Saturday** Samedi	**January** Janvier	**May** Mai	**September** Septembre
Tuesday Mardi	**Sunday** Dimanche	**February** Février	**June** Juin	**October** Octobre
Wednesday Mercredi	**Today** Aujourd'hui	**March** Mars	**July** Juillet	**November** Novembre
Thursday Jeudi	**Tomorrow** Demain	**April** Avril	**August** Août	**December** Décembre
Friday Vendredi	**Yesterday** Hier			

Restaurant
Restaurant

FOOD & DRINK

Change Monnaie	**English menu** Menu anglais	**High chair** Chaise haute	**The check** L'addition

I'd like to take it home
J'aimerais l'emporter

I'll have your recommendation
J'aimerais avoir la suggestion du chef

I'll have what they're having
J'aimerais avoir la même chose que ces personnes

I'm a vegetarian
Je suis végétarien(ne)

I'm allergic to...
Je suis allergique…

Eggs
Aux œufs

Milk
Au lait

Peanuts
Aux cacahuètes

Sesame seeds
Aux graines de sésame

Shellfish
Aux crustacés

Soy
Au soja

Tree nuts
Aux fruits secs

Wheat
Au blé

This dish is...
Ce plat est…

Delicious
Délicieux

Too cold
Trop froid

Too hot
Trop chaud

Too spicy
Trop épicé

FOOD & DRINK • HELP

Drinking glass
Verre

Napkin
Serviette

Plate **Bowl**
Assiette Bol

Silverware
Couverts

No cheese
Sans fromage

No meat or poultry
Sans viande ou volaille

No peanuts
Sans cacahuète

No seafood
Sans fruits de mer

Balsamic vinegar
Vinaigre balsamique

Ketchup
Ketchup

Lemon wedges
Tranches de citron

Mayonnaise
Mayonnaise

Mustard
Moutarde

Olive oil
Huile d'olive

Red wine vinegar
Vinaigre de vin rouge

White wine vinegar
Vinaigre de vin blanc

FOOD & DRINK • HELP

Butter \ Beurre	Honey \ Miel	Jam \ Confiture	Syrup \ Sirop
Salt Pepper \ Sel Poivre	Sugar \ Sucre	Sugar substitute \ Édulcorant	Toothpick \ Cure-dent

**Black tea /
Herbal tea**
Thé noir / Infusion

Bottled water
Eau en
bouteille

**Coffee /
Coffee with milk**
Café / Café au lait

Iced tea
Thé glacé

Juice
Jus

Lemonade
Citronnade

Milk
Lait

Soda
Coca

FOOD & DRINK • HELP

Beer	Red wine	White wine	Ice
Bière	Vin rouge	Vin blanc	Glaçons
Gin & tonic	Rum & coke	Vodka & soda	Vodka & tonic
Gin tonic	Rhum Coca	Vodka eau de seltz	Vodka tonic

Petit-déjeuner
Breakfast

FOOD & DRINK • BREAKFAST

Apple turnover	Chausson aux pommes
Bread with butter & jam	Tartine
Croissant	Croissant
Glazed roll filled with custard & raisins	Pain aux raisins
Pastry with chocolate inside	Pain au chocolat
Slightly sweet, light bread	Pain au lait
Sweet, flaky bread	Brioche

En-cas

Snacks

FOOD & DRINK • SNACKS

Cheese soufflé	Soufflé au fromage
Egg tart with bacon & cheese	Quiche Lorraine
Grilled ham & cheese sandwich	Croque-monsieur
Grilled ham & cheese sandwich with a fried egg	Croque-madame
Hamburger & fries in a baguette	Sandwich Américain
Sandwich with ham & butter	Sandwich jambon-beurre
Sandwich with ham & cheese	Sandwich jambon-fromage
Sandwich with cheese	Sandwich fromage
Sandwich with chicken	Sandwich poulet
Sandwich with tuna	Sandwich thon
Sandwich with tuna, egg, & olives	Pain bagnat

Entrées

Appetizers

FOOD & DRINK • APPETIZERS

Crouton rounds with toppings	Canapés
Egg cooked in a ramekin with cream	Œuf cocotte
Marinated olives	Olives marinées
Salad with bacon, Roquefort cheese, & walnuts	Salade Aveyronaise
Salad with tuna, egg, vegetables, & olives	Salade Niçoise
Vegetables with a vinaigrette dressing	Assiette de crudités

Soup

Leek & potato soup	Soupe aux poireaux et pommes de terre
Onion soup	Soupe à l'oignon
Vegetable & bean soup with basil-garlic sauce	Soupe au pistou

Plat principal
Main course

FOOD & DRINK • MAIN COURSE

Chicken & mushrooms braised in red wine	Coq au vin
Duck leg, salt-cured & poached in fat	Confit de canard
Duck with orange sauce	Canard à l'orange
Lamb or mutton stew	Navarin
Poached fish in white wine	Filets de poisson pochés au vin blanc
Roasted chicken	Poulet rôti
Stew of beef braised in red wine	Bœuf Bourguignon
Stew of tomatoes & other vegetables	Ratatouille
Steak with fries	Steak frites
Steak with pepper & cognac cream sauce	Steak au poivre
White bean casserole with meat & sausages	Cassoulet

Dessert

Desserts

FOOD & DRINK • DESSERTS

Cheese plate	Assiette de fromages
Cherries or other fruit baked in a cake	Clafoutis
Chocolate cake with chocolate filling	Fondant au chocolat
Chocolate custard cup	Pot de crème au chocolat
Chocolate mousse	Mousse au chocolat
Cream puffs	Choux à la crème
Crepes with orange sauce	Crêpes Suzette
Custard flan with a caramel sauce	Crème caramel
Fruit tarts	Tartes aux fruits
Puff pastry layered with cream (napolean)	Mille-feuille
Upside-down apple tart	Tarte tatin

Préparez-moi un plat avec…

Please cook me a dish with…

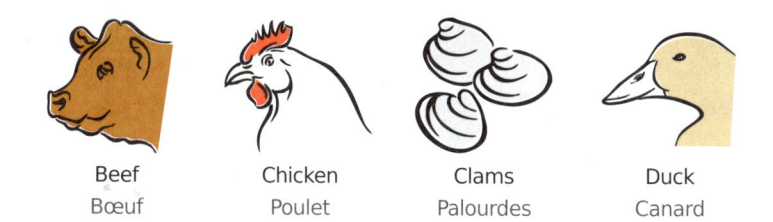

Beef
Bœuf

Chicken
Poulet

Clams
Palourdes

Duck
Canard

FOOD & DRINK • MEAT &

Fish	**Lamb**	**Mussels**	**Oysters**
Poisson	Agneau	Moules	Huîtres
Pork	**Rabbit**	**Shrimp**	**Squid**
Porc	Lapin	Crevettes	Calmar

SEAFOOD

Préparez-moi un plat avec…

Please cook me a dish with…

Artichokes
Artichauts

Asparagus
Asperges

Beets
Betteraves

Broccoli
Brocoli

FOOD & DRINK • VEGETABLES

Bell pepper Poivron	**Cabbage** Chou	**Carrots** Carottes	**Cauliflower** Chou-fleur
Celery Céleri	**Corn** Maïs	**Cucumber** Concombre	**Eggplant** Aubergine

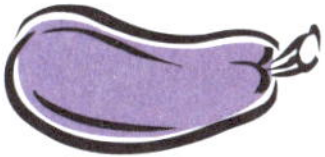

Préparez-moi un plat avec...

Please cook me a dish with...

Garlic
Ail

Green beans
Haricots verts

Leeks
Poireaux

Lettuce
Laitue

FOOD & DRINK • VEGETABLES

Mushrooms Champignons	**Olives** Olives	**Onion** Oignon	**Peas** Pois
Potatoes Pommes de terre	**Spinach** Épinards	**Tomatoes** Tomates	**Zucchini** Courgette

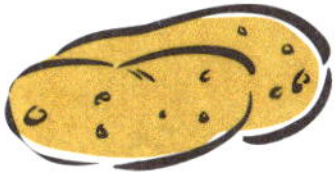

Apple
Pomme

Apricot
Abricot

Bananas
Bananes

Blackberries
Mûres

Blackcurrant
Cassis

Cherries
Cerises

Grapefruit
Pamplemousse

Grapes
Raisins

FOOD & DRINK • FRUIT

Orange Orange	**Peach** Pêche	**Pear** Poire	**Plums** Prunes
Raspberries Framboises	**Strawberries** Fraises	**Tangerine** Mandarine	**Watermelon** Pastèque

Aéroport
Airport

GETTING AROUND · AIR

Arrival gate	Hall d'arrivée
Departure gate	Hall de départ
Domestic terminal	Terminal national
International terminal	Terminal international
I need to change my reservation	Je dois changer ma réservation
My luggage is damaged	Mes bagages sont endommagés
My luggage is lost	Mes bagages sont perdus
Where is the airport shuttle?	Où se trouve la navette de l'aéroport ?
Where is the ticket counter?	Où se trouve le comptoir de vente des billets ?

Baggage claim
Retrait des bagages

Customs
Douane

Immigration
Immigration

Information desk
Guichet des renseignements

GETTING AROUND • CAR

Location de voiture
Car rental

Budget rental	Location à petit budget
Standard rental	Location standard
4-wheel drive rental	Location d'un 4X4
Automatic	Boîte automatique
Manual	Boîte manuelle

Fill it up, please	Le plein, s'il vous plait
How much is it per hour?	Quel est le tarif horaire ?
How much is it per day?	Quel est le tarif pour la journée ?
How much is it overnight?	Quel est le tarif pour la nuit ?
I need air in the tires	J'ai besoin de faire la pression des pneus
Is it safe to park here?	Peut-on se garer ici en toute sécurité ?

One way
Aller simple

Round trip
Aller-retour

Insurance
Assurance

Child car seat
Siège auto pour enfant

RENTAL

Taxi

I need a taxi now	J'ai besoin d'un taxi maintenant	**Today**	Aujourd'hui
I need a taxi at…(time)	J'ai besoin d'un taxi aujourd'hui à…	**Tomorrow**	Demain
I need a taxi tomorrow at…(time)	J'ai besoin d'un taxi demain à…	**One way**	Aller simple
		Round trip	Aller-retour
How much does it cost?	Combien cela coûte-t-il ?		
Please drive faster	Pouvez-vous rouler plus vite ?		
Please drive slower	Pouvez-vous rouler moins vite ?		
Please stop here	Arrêtez-vous là, s'il vous plait		
Please use the meter	Laissez tourner le compteur		
Please wait for me	Attendez-moi		

Gare
Train station

High speed train	TGV
Local train	Train régional
Long distance train	Train longue distance
Overnight train	Train de nuit

I have a reservation	J'ai réservé
Is this train going to…?	Est-ce que ce train va à… ?
When does the train arrive?	À quelle heure arrive ce train ?
When does the train leave?	À quelle heure part ce train ?
When is the last train?	À quelle heure est le dernier train ?
When is the next train?	À quelle heure est le prochain train ?

First class
Première classe

Second class
Deuxième classe

Upper berth
Couchette du haut

Middle berth
Couchette du milieu

Lower berth
Couchette du bas

One way
Aller simple

Round trip
Aller-retour

Bicycle	**Boat**
Vélo	Bateau

Bus	**Car**
Bus	Voiture

Ferry	**Motorbike**
Ferry	Moto

Parking lot	**Subway**
Parking	Métro

GETTING AROUND • HELP

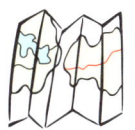

Flat tire	Gas (petrol)	Mechanic	Tow truck
Pneu crevé	Essence	Mécanicien	Dépanneuse

Map	Tickets	Compass	North Nord
Carte	Billets	Boussole	South Sud
			East Est
			West Ouest

Art gallery
Galerie d'art

Bar
Bar

Beach
Plage

Cathedral
Cathédrale

Embassy
Ambassade

Hair salon
Coiffeur

Internet cafe
Cybercafé

Movie theater
Cinéma

GETTING AROUND • HELP

Museum	**Night club**	**Park**	**Post office**
Musée	Boîte de nuit	Parc	Bureau de poste
Spa	**Sports stadium**	**Street market**	**Travel agency**
Spa	Stade	Marché	Agence de voyage

ACCOMMODATION

Hôtel
Hotel

Bed & breakfast
Chambre d'hôte

Budget hotel
Hôtel économique

Hostel
Auberge

Upscale hotel
Hôtel haut de gamme

Do you have a room?
Avez-vous une chambre ?

May I see the room?
Puis-je voir la chambre ?

I want to extend my stay
J'aimerais prolonger mon séjour

Show me your cheapest room
Montrez-moi votre chambre la moins chère

How much is it...
Quel est le tarif...

Per night?
Pour la nuit ?

Per week?
Pour la semaine ?

Per month?
Pour le mois ?

May I have a discount?
Pouvez-vous me faire
une remise ?

There's a problem...
Il y a un problème...

With the lighting
Avec la lumière

With the key
Avec la clé

With the shower
Avec la douche

With the toilet
Avec les toilettes

One week
Une semaine

Two weeks
Deux semaines

Three weeks
Trois semaines

One month
Un mois

Deposit
Acompte

Reservation
Réservation

ACCOMMODATION • HELP

Can I checkout late?
Est-il possible de libérer la chambre tard ?

I lost my key
J'ai perdu ma clé

I need a password for the Internet
J'ai besoin d'un mot de passe pour Internet

I'd like to change my room
J'aimerais changer de chambre

Is there a curfew?
Y a-t-il un couvre-feu ?

May I have a name card (business card)?
Puis-je avoir une carte de visite ?

Quiet please!
Un peu de silence, s'il vous plait !

When is checkout?
À quelle heure faut-il libérer la chambre ?

Hot water
Eau chaude

Cold water
Eau froide

Too noisy
Trop bruyant(e)

Too pricey
Trop cher/chère

Too cold
Trop froid(e)

Too warm
Trop chaud(e)

Too dirty
Trop sale

Air con Air conditionné	**Alarm clock** Réveil	**Baby crib** Lit pour enfant	**Babysitting** Baby-sitting
Blanket Couverture	**Business center** Centre d'affaires	**Concierge** Concierge	**Conditioner** Après-shampooing

ACCOMMODATION • HELP

Fan	Fitness center	Hair dryer	Housekeeping
Ventilateur	Centre de remise en forme	Sèche-cheveux	Ménage
In-room internet	Key	Laundry	Left luggage
Internet dans les chambres	Clé	Laverie	Consigne

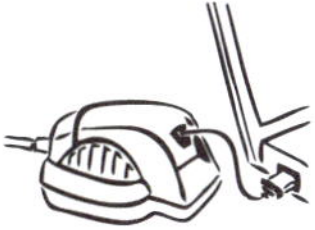

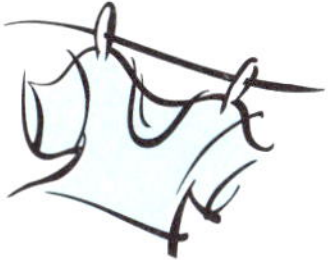

Massage
Massage

Moisturizing lotion
Lotion hydratante

Non-smoking room
Chambre non fumeur

Pillow
Oreiller

Porter
Portier

Private bath
Salle de bain privée

Room service
Service d'étage

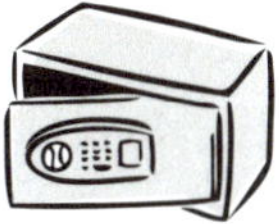

Safe
Coffre

ACCOMMODATION • HELP

Satellite TV	Shampoo	Sheets	Soap
TV satellite	Shampooing	Draps	Savon
Toilet paper	Towel	Wake-up call	Wifi access
Papier toilette	Serviette	Service de réveil	Accès Wifi

Centre commercial

Shopping mall

Bakery	**Book store**	**Camera store**	**Clothing store**
Boulangerie	Librairie	Magasin d'appareils photo	Magasin de vêtements

How much does it cost?
Combien cela coûte t-il ?

I'd like to try this on
J'aimerais l'essayer

I'd like to exchange this item
J'aimerais échanger cet article

Please give me a refund
Remboursez-moi, s'il vous plait

Belt
Ceinture

Boots
Bottes

Bra
Soutien-gorge

Dress / Skirt
Robe / Jupe

Flip flops
Tongs

Gloves
Gants

Jacket
Veste

Knit Hat
Bonnet

SHOPPING • APPAREL

Shirt	Shoes	Socks	Sun hat
Chemise	Chaussures	Chaussettes	Chapeau de soleil
Swimming suit	Trousers / Shorts	Umbrella	Underwear
Maillot de bain	Pantalon / Shorts	Parapluie	Sous-vêtements

Bandages	Cotton swabs	Dental floss	Deodorant
Bandages	Coton-tiges	Fil dentaire	Déodorant

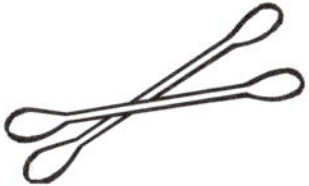

Eye drops	Lip balm	Moisturizing lotion	Mosquito repellent
Gouttes ophtalmiques	Baume à lèvres	Lotion hydratante	Anti-moustiques

SHOPPING • PERSONAL CARE

Razor	Shampoo / Conditioner	Shaving cream	Soap
Rasoir	Shampooing / Après-shampooing	Crème à raser	Savon
Sunscreen	Tissues	Toothbrush / Paste	Tweezers
Crème solaire	Mouchoirs	Brosse à dents / Dentifrice	Pince à épiler

Alarm clock
Réveil

Batteries
Piles

Beach towel
Serviette
de plage

Blank CD / DVD
CD / DVD vierge

Camera film
Pellicule

Ear plugs
Bouchons
d'oreille

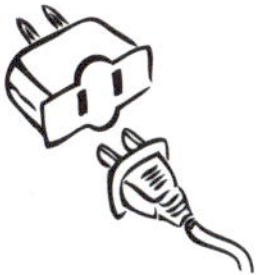

Electricity adaptor
Adaptateur pour
prise électrique

English book
Livre
en anglais

SHOPPING • SUNDRIES

Eye mask	**Flashlight**	**Memory card**	**Note pad**
Masque oculaire	Lampe de poche	Carte mémoire	Bloc-notes
Padlock	**Playing cards**	**Sewing kit**	**Sunglasses**
Cadenas	Cartes à jouer	Nécessaire de couture	Lunettes de soleil

Baby aspirin
Aspirine
infantile

Baby bonnet
Bonnet
pour bébé

Baby bottle
Biberon

Baby carrier
Porte-bébé

Baby food
Aliments
pour bébé

Baby formula
Lait infantile

Baby wipes
Lingettes
pour bébé

Bib
Bavette

SHOPPING • BABY

Blanket	**Bottle nipple**	**Diapers**	**Diaper rash cream**
Couverture	Tétine pour biberon	Couches	Crème anti-érythème fessier
Pacifier	**Powder**	**Stroller**	**Toys**
Tétine	Talc	Poussette	Jouets

White	Gray	Black	Brown
Blanc	Gris	Noir	Marron

Red	Red-orange	Orange	Yellow-orange
Rouge	Rouge-orange	Orange	Jaune-orange

SHOPPING • COLORS

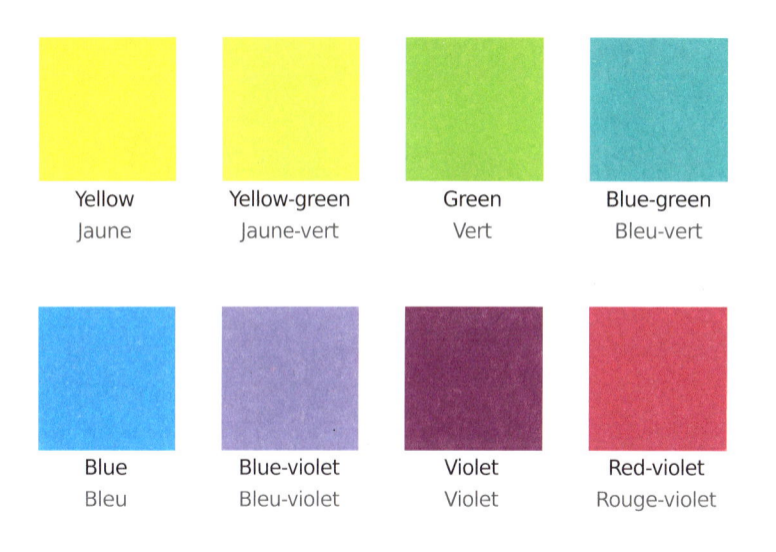

Yellow Jaune	Yellow-green Jaune-vert	Green Vert	Blue-green Bleu-vert
Blue Bleu	Blue-violet Bleu-violet	Violet Violet	Red-violet Rouge-violet

HEALTH & SAFETY

Hôpital
Hospital

Dentist	Doctor	Pharmacist	Police
Dentiste	Docteur	Pharmacien	Police

I feel ill
Je ne me sens pas bien

I want to contact my embassy
Je veux contacter mon ambassade

I have travel insurance
J'ai une assurance de voyage

I'm lost
Je suis perdu(e)

I lost my...
J'ai perdu
mon/ma/mes…

ATM card
Carte de débit

Back pack / Purse
Sac à dos / Sac à main

Camera
Appareil photo

Credit card
Carte de crédit

Someone stole my...
On m'a volé
mon/ma/mes…

Luggage
Bagages

Passport
Passeport

Travelers checks
Chèques de voyage

Wallet
Portefeuille

Medicine

Antacid
Antiacide

Antibacterial cream
Crème
antibactérienne

Antibiotics
Antibiotique

Aspirin
Aspirine

Diarrhea medicine
Anti-diarrhéique

Pain killers
Anti-douleur

HEALTH & SAFETY • HELP

I've been..
J'ai été…

Attacked
Attaqué(e)

Injured
Blessé(e)

Raped
Violé(e)

Robbed
Dévalisé(e)

I'm allergic to...
Je suis allergique…

Bee stings
Aux piqûres d'abeilles

Cats / Dogs
Aux chats / Aux chiens

Penicillin
À la pénicilline

Pollen
Au pollen

Personal

Birth control pills
Pilule contraceptive

Condoms
Préservatifs

Contact lenses
Lentilles de contact

Sanitary napkins
Serviettes hygiéniques

Tampons
Tampons

I need medicine for...
J'ai besoin d'un médicament pour...

A bladder infection
Une cystite

A cold
Un rhume

A toothache
Une rage de dent

A yeast infection
Une infection
aux levures

Anxiety
L'anxiété

Athlete's foot
Un pied d'athlète

Flu
La grippe

Food poisoning
Une intoxication
alimentaire

I have...
Je souffre...

AIDS
Du SIDA

Asthma
D'asthme

Cancer
D'un cancer

Diabetes
De diabète

Epilepsy
D'épilepsie

HEALTH & SAFETY · HELP

Symptoms:
Symptômes :

Chills	Dizziness	Nausea
Refroidissements	Vertiges	Nausée
Constipation	Ear ache	Sore throat
Constipation	Mal d'oreille	Mal de gorge
Cramps	Fever	Stuffy nose
Crampes	Fièvre	Nez bouché
Diarrhea	Headache	Swelling
Diarrhée	Mal de tête	Gonflement

Altitude sickness	**Blister**
Mal des montagnes	Ampoule

Car accident	**Dehydration**
Accident de voiture	Déshydratation

Dog bite	**Fire**
Morsure de chien	Incendie

Heat stroke	**Heart attack**
Coup de chaleur	Crise cardiaque

HEALTH & SAFETY · HELP

Overdose	Sprained ankle / wrist	Sunburn	Toothache
Overdose	Entorse de la cheville / du poignée	Coup de soleil	Rage de dent
No blood transfusion	No IV	No needle	No tooth extraction
Pas de transfusion sanguine	Pas d'IV	Pas d'aiguille	Pas d'extraction dentaire